*Flowers for the Living*

*Fairchild Family 1913*

Back Row: Stella, Kirby, Wallace, and Cady.

Front Row: Virgil, JW, Lucile, Lyda, Juanita (On Lap), and Leonard

# Flowers for the Living: Honey for the Trail from Great-Grandfather

JW Fairchild

Edited by David Fado

Preface by Don Fado

Contributions from
Donna Fado Ivery, Carolyn Fado and Elizabeth Fado

Illustrations by Kaitlyn Fado

Our Orbs Publishing

*Swirls from the start of the Oregon Trail*

Our Orbs Publishing

Copyright © 2019 by David Fado and the Fado-Fairchild Family.

All rights reserved. This book or any portion thereof may not be reproduced or used in any manner whatsoever without the express written permission of the publisher except for the use of brief quotations in a book review or scholarly journal.

First Printing: 2019

ISBN 978-1-950893-01-0

Our Orbs
PO Box 7522
Arlington, VA 22207

Our Orbs Publishing focuses on the core elements that make up our communities and publishes positive contributions across multiple media platforms. Our Orbs includes the solid elements of humanity and spirit that keep us together. As JW Fairchild writes, **"Inertia and gravitation were inherent in matter when the first orb was rolled out into space, and they perform their functions unerringly today."**

www.ourorbs.com

# Dedication

This book is dedicated to all families who came to America and dedicated their life to the vision of a world that lives up to the principles of Jesus

# Contents

Acknowledgments .................................................................................... ix

Trail Guide ............................................................................................... x

Preface ..................................................................................................... xi

    Reverend Don Fado, Grandson ........................................................ xi

Introduction ............................................................................................. 1

Flowers for the Living .............................................................................. 7

    Original Text ...................................................................................... 7

    Trail Notes 1:  Deeds and Acts as Flowers ...................................... 9

Are You Old ............................................................................................ 13

    Original Text .................................................................................... 13

    Trails Notes 2:  Age Quiz ................................................................ 15

Soul Hunger ............................................................................................ 17

    Original Text .................................................................................... 17

    Trail Notes 3:  Quilt for the Soul .................................................... 19

Change and the Changeless ................................................................... 21

    Original Text .................................................................................... 21

    Trail Notes 4:  Elizabeth Fado, Great-Great-Granddaughter ........ 23

Predestination ........................................................................................ 25

    Original Text .................................................................................... 25

    Trail Notes 5:  Maps of a Planned Trip .......................................... 34

Struggle—The Price of Victory .............................................................. 37

    Original Text .................................................................................... 37

    Trail Notes 6:  Out of Struggle, Beauty in Utah ............................. 39

Robbing God ........................................................................................... 41

    Original Text .................................................................................... 41

| | |
|---|---|
| Trail Notes 7: The Great Gifts of Creation | 43 |
| **Happiness** | **45** |
| Original Text | 45 |
| Trail Notes 8: Carolyn Fado, Great-Great-Granddaughter | 48 |
| **"But if Not"** | **51** |
| Original Text | 51 |
| Trail Notes 9: Donna Fado Ivery, Great-Granddaughter | 54 |
| **A Little Bit of Honey** | **55** |
| Original Text | 55 |
| Trail Notes 10: Humor Keeps the Edge | 58 |
| **Why Serve God** | **59** |
| Original Text | 59 |
| Trail Notes 11: For the Love of Creation | 62 |
| **The Christian Warfare** | **63** |
| Original Text | 63 |
| Interlude: Kentucky Gourds | 74 |
| Original Text | 74 |
| Trail Notes 12: Achievements | 81 |
| **About the Editor and Contributors** | **85** |

# Acknowledgments

I thank my grandmother, Lucile Fado for giving me the stack of papers that led to this book. May the love of her father and the love she gave to all her children find their reflection in the work here.

*Lucile Fado with one of her children.*

*Lucile Fado with Don and Great-Granddaughter Elizabeth Fado.*

# Trail Guide

This volume includes the original writings of JW Fairchild under the heading "original text." Additional thoughts, pictures and drawings are included under trail notes.

This edition includes the following convention for text color

Black Text: Material from the original manuscript and notes from the editor.

**Purple Text: Quotations from the Bible.**

**Whiskey Color: Quotations from the JW Fairchild manuscript outside the original text sections.**

**Blue Text: Special writings and quotations from descendants of JW Fairchild.**

Where possible I have maintained the original text. Where JW quoted the bible but assumed his reader would know the verse, I have added in the verse. For the final say on any confusing bible quotes, I followed JW in using the King James Version.

Many of these writings come from the first half of the last century, so they do not follow many of today's conventions.

# Preface

Reverend Don Fado, Grandson

When I was a child growing up in Pennsylvania, my family tried to visit all my grandparents once a year. We lived 600 miles from Whitesburg, Kentucky where the Fairchilds lived, and another 900 miles from Wichita, Kansas where the Fados lived. These were long trips, but my mother and father stayed close to their families and took us along with them. Roads were harsh and motels rare so we stayed in a variety of tourist homes on these trips.

World War II changed all of that. Gas was rationed, and we moved to California when my dad became Circulation Manager of the Redding newspaper. I recall only seeing Grandpa Fairchild a couple of times after the war. My sister and I were teenagers and the Fairchilds lived in Texarkana, Texas, over 2,000 miles away. We next saw him when my wife Jeanie, my mother and I visited grandpa and Grandma Lyda as part of a cross country drive in 1956. Jeanie and I were newlyweds on our way to seminary in Boston while my mom stayed over with her parents for an extended visit.

We stayed a couple of days and grandpa had me preach at his church. It was only about the 3$^{rd}$ sermon I ever preached. It was a Missionary Baptist Church. They shouted "amen" – Jeanie said I became monotone because every time I inflected my voice an amen came from the congregation. I was not comfortable with it then; I would love such interaction and encouragement now. Grandpa had been an evangelist most of his ministry. He was also editor of a national publication of the Missionary Baptists. Mother said she hardly knew him as she grew up: "He was gone most of the time and then came home and got momma pregnant again and was gone."

Grandpa's heart was calcifying. He took a tablespoon of whiskey every so often to stimulate it. He said Baptists allow whiskey as long as it is medicinal, which means you have to use a spoon to ingest it. He added as he licked his lips, "I really like that stuff." That was the first time I really had an adult conversation with grandpa. We talked and talked. He quoted Paul, "Woe to me if I do not preach the gospel" which was a part of his very being and purpose in life. He told me that his favorite book was *How to Believe* by Ralph Sockman, a Methodist.

I had heard Sockman preach at a student conference and had read one of his books of sermons. He was clearly a liberal theologian. This amazed me as grandpa was part of a very conservative church. They did not even allow musical instruments in the worship service. He told me that he felt God wanted him to be in that church because he was needed there. I found him to be loving, caring and open. I wish I had had the opportunity to get to know him more fully. It would be the last time I would see him.

In my Introduction to the Old Testament class during my first semester we were required to write a paper that would be at least 100 pages long: the professor would lecture on the history and we would study and write about each of the 39 books of the Old Testament telling its background, authorship, place in history, etc. I had never written a paper over 12 pages in my life. It was a major challenge. I felt it was a book in itself. I dedicated it to Joseph Fairchild, my grandfather. I was not sure how he would feel about it; my presentation was that there was an evolution in understanding the nature of God beginning with the very primitive, vindictive being (God walking in the Garden of Eden and casting out Adam & Eve) and evolving into the God of love of all creation as in the prophets, a far cry from biblical literalists.

He wrote me a letter telling me how thrilled he was to see me starting out where he left off. He had come to the same understanding of scripture toward the end of his life through living life and studying the scriptures. He had never attended seminary. He saw me carrying on and going even further in understanding the nature of God. That letter was precious to me. I regret I have lost the letter, but I shall never lose its message.

It is too late for me to tell him how he enriched my life. After he died, mother gave me his sermon notebook where he had poems, quotes, etc. I was startled to read many of the same things I have used in my sermons. We were attracted to the same truth. As he says, "Flowers should be given while people are alive… when the recipient can have the joy of knowing that he (sic) is remembered." I didn't send him any bouquets in his lifetime, other than the visit and paper, but I shall continue to express thanks for his life.

Don Fado

October 2018

*Recreation of a 1930s tourist house from the Lincoln Trail*

*A flower from Kaitlyn*

## Introduction

This book comes from a manuscript my great-grandfather, JW Fairchild submitted to a New York publisher in 1955 at the age of 84. Nana Fado, my grandmother and JW's daughter, gave me the manuscript in 2002, shortly before she passed away. Nana told me how her father worked long and hard on his writings and that she knew I would figure out something to do with her father's thoughts.

Church shaped my Nana and she proudly recognized the tradition of preaching within her family. Her son, Don Fado, is a minister along with her granddaughters, Lyda Pierce and Donna Fado Ivery. She also added two preachers by marriage, as Donna and Lyda both married ministers. With all that preaching in the family, I am not sure why she blessed me with her father's writings, but she did. I stored them and considered how to keep them safe.

The manuscript on hundreds of yellowing typewritten pages was tucked into the self-addressed stamped envelope with very cool 1950s stamps that JW provided the publisher. In addition to the manuscript, the publisher included a polite rejection letter. I scanned these typewritten pages and put them out as a photo book. This produced a clunky and huge coffee table tome for the family that preserved the writings but proved difficult to read. I did not engage with his thoughts but there they stayed for years until I was asked by a family member to consider putting the writings out in eBook format, as the scanned images proved difficult to read and the hardcover book came at a high price tag.

I talked with JW's great-great granddaughter, Carolyn Fado about making an eBook with Optical Character Recognition (OCR) scanning, but the handwritten annotations proved too hard to translate. We agreed that someone would need to re-type the manuscript to put it out as an eBook. That task remained until I reviewed my photo archives in 2018 and I decided to start typing.

# JW Fairchild

The highlight of the 2018 Summer was a big car ride for the younger girls and my wife from Chicago to California. Originally sold to my 12 and 13-year-old daughters (Kaitlyn and Elizabeth) as the "human Oregon Trail adventures," this soon became known as "Trail Trek 2018" complete with tour T-Shirt. Taking the Trail Trek with the old manuscript along for the ride provided a new perspective. Suddenly I had another companion on the trail who better understood the struggles those early pioneers faced. Grandma had told me I would do something with her father's thoughts; I did not know it would take this trek for me to understand them. As I absorbed his wisdom on our trip, I decided a simple reproduction of the text from great-grandfather Fairchild's life would do little justice to the vitality and vigor with which he approached the gospel, God and building a life for his family and future generations.

Who was my great-grandfather? His writings preserve his vision and paint a striking portrait of a practical man with the strength it took to fashion Christian communities on the frontier. He was a great companion on Trail Trek 2018, even better than recorded audio of Harry Potter or the Hunger Games.

The foreword provided in the 1955 manuscript by J. Gladston Emery provides a first-hand description of JW Fairchild as follows: "As other hardy pioneers, his first schooling was in the familiar log cabin, however he had a yearning for learning and absorbed knowledge. At the age of fourteen he donned his first 'store-bought' suit to wear to teach at a rural school; at the age of eighteen he was considered one of the most learned teachers in the rural mountain section and was looked to as an authority on Scriptures…it was then he started his preaching career that has carried him from pulpit to pulpit for over a half century." In short, "he has been carrying The Word from congregation to individual throughout half of the states of the Union—he is now busily engaged with a pastorate and his writings leading a most active life."

*Flowers for the Living*

In 2018, well over sixty years after his death, I typed his manuscript as we followed the path of earlier pioneers. His thoughts took on a new dimension as we recognized the intense day to day struggle just to cross the country that JW and generations just before him had. At the start of the trail, a museum showed us the abandoned possessions that became too heavy for those travelers. I considered the life of JW Fairchild, who lived in harsh conditions and tossed aside luxurious ideas in favor of a spirituality needed to nourish him through the challenges of survival. These hundreds of sheets contained his wisdom for me and his family. I became very interested in what I could find out about his book.

I ran a search on JW Fairchild and found preserved in Google a lively 1910 debate about predestination that split the primitive Baptist church at the time. Most of the church held firmly against any notion of predestination, and JW Fairchild seemed to enjoy bringing up the counter argument. One Baptist minister blamed the young JW Fairchild for the conflict, writing that JW Fairchild's advocacy of predestination "is what causes the division."[1] My great-grandfather did not mince words about the debate over predestination. C.H. Cayce quotes JW as saying **"Our labors with these elders who are bent on dividing the Lord's people over predestination and time salvation are at an end; and hereafter our efforts shall be to save the flock from their tyranny."** Predestination disagreements among primitive Baptists provided some unexpected lively exchanges.

JW Fairchild's advocacy showed a love for the planner, stressing that God had a program and did not leave all to chance. **"If finite man would not build a house without deciding beforehand what kind of house he was going to build and the purpose that house was to serve, would the Infinite God, with whom are hid all the treasures of wisdom and knowledge, create a world with all that is in it, without deciding beforehand what kind of a world he was going to**

---

[1] C.H. Cayce, *Editorial Writing from the Primitive Baptist, 1896-1910,* New York: Lulu.com, p. 178.

**create and what purpose that world would fulfill?"** For JW Fairchild, God had planned the world and our role as preachers of the gospel was to build the best world we could, in spite of all the pain and suffering that may occur along the trail.

The passion for progress, life and vision came through in these writings. I retyped JW's words not only as a way to store a memory, I started a conversation that brought thought to life and captured a vision. The conversation with JW Fairchild continued on the trip. I retyped essays that spoke to me through the great plains, the salt flats and the towering mountains. The Oregon Trail journey is easy now in a car, but still today the rugged nature of the pioneers who tamed this land comes through, and that spirit glows in JW's writings. While the physical journey now glides easily over rubber tires and asphalt roads, our spiritual journey remains just as difficult, if not more so, today. Great-grandfather made it clear in his writing that the strivings of the soul were the real mark of our success in life. JW himself never crossed the entire Oregon Trail, but his life in Tennessee, Kansas, Kentucky and Arkansas from the nineteenth century into the twentieth provided me insight into those pioneers I got nowhere else. The trail provided a backdrop that led to a new appreciation for his writings about God, struggle and family.

The essay "Flowers for the Living" convinced me that my great-grandfather would want to share his thoughts with the living, not bury those thoughts with the dead. Therefore, I decided to add "trail notes" and this preface inspired by these essays. The great spirit JW showed for life well into his eighties convinced me that he was a man who wanted his thoughts to impact those in his community: **"In the hour of distress, when all your ambitions have been crushed, your hopes blighted, your faith gone, and the future holds out nothing to you but dark despair, nothing can revive the despondent spirit, restore faith, and bring back hope, like the assurance that someone cares."**

## *Flowers for the Living*

JW Fairchild shared his thoughts and vision on paper as part of his active life. He had no chance to post on Instagram or create a story on Snapchat, but I think he would have loved those opportunities to share his vision and preach the gospel. We do, however, have these essays from another time.

During the Summer I made my way through about half of his essays. I confess, until I allowed them to steep in my thoughts, the pages remained as dry leaves with no life or nourishment. Are these ideas and thoughts old? If left on the paper without thought, yes. As part of a conversation, they became something more.

JW Fairchild

*Flowers from the start of the Oregon Trail*

# Flowers for the Living

## Original Text

When our friends pass on we place flowers on their caskets as a token of our love and appreciation. This is well. It would be ungrateful to bury our friends without an expression of the esteem in which they are held. You and I would hate to know that no one would place a flower or sprig of green on our grave when our body sleeps the sleep of death.

But our zeal in heaping flowers on the graves of our departed friends often runs to the extreme. In honoring the dead we sometimes forget the living. I have known people to spend large sums of money on flowers for a departed husband when his widow and children were left in dire need. A few flowers for the departed, and help for the bereaved family, would be more in keeping with the spirit of Christ. The dead have no needs; the living have many.

Flowers should be given while people are alive and can appreciate their fragrance and beauty. And especially they should be given when the recipient can have the joy of knowing that he is remembered. Why wait to send your flowers till your friend is dead, and can neither see their beauty nor smell their fragrance, nor even know that you still remember him? Flowers are worth far more to people while they are living and can appreciate them, than they are piled on their grave when dead.

Think what flowers may mean to the living. By flowers I mean also words of encouragement, acts of kindness, deeds of love and service.

In the hour of distress, when all your ambitions have been crushed, your hopes blighted, your faith gone, and the future holds out nothing to you but dark despair, nothing can revive the despondent spirit, restore faith, and bring back hope, like the assurance that someone cares.

Just to know that someone is interested in you; someone is praying for your success, makes life worth living. But if you are interested in some one, if you want to lend a helping hand, but you never let him know it, what will it benefit him? Don't fail to give your flowers when you see their need.

Yes, give flowers to the living. If you like a person, or love him, tell him now. If you admire what he is doing, and appreciate his course in life, let him know it. Do not wait till his ear is cold in death and cannot hear what you say, then sing his praises and heap flowers on his coffin. We cannot appreciate it then, and your good offices will be in vain.

We are all human enough to appreciate a word of praise. To know that your labors are appreciated by others, that your words and acts revive the spirit of those with whom you came into contact, gives zest to life, and inspires you to greater effort in the work you are doing. And other people are like you. If their words of praise and appreciation help you, yours will help them. So do unto them as you would have them do unto you.

Yes, place a few flowers on my casket when I am gone if you will, but please hand me a few now while I can enjoy their fragrance and beauty.

*Flowers for the Living*

## Trail Notes 1: Deeds and Acts as Flowers

As I completed the retype of "Flowers for the Living," my youngest daughter, Kaitlyn, asked what I was doing. I had her draw a flower for her ancestors. That flower is in this book right after the Preface.

JW observes that **"if you are interested in some one, if you want to lend a helping hand, but you never let him know it, what will it benefit him? Don't fail to give your flowers when you see their need."** How can we give these flowers? Simply ordering from the internet provides no **"words of encouragement, acts of kindness, deeds of love and service."** Such a gift must come from the heart, so flower services allow for a handwritten note to accompany the delivery. We need a flower and personal notes for Instagram and Snapchat.

I considered how to send such a personal note and decided to take the flower Kaitlyn drew and use it as a template for these words of encouragement and acts of kindness. I decided to make one for my father and wrote out my appreciation for him on the petals. That flower is shown at the end of this chapter. Go ahead and post one for a loved one!

Trail Trek included many monuments to Abraham Lincoln. The Lincoln library included wax replicas of Lincoln and his family across various stages of his life. We loved playing with these wax figures, as they captured a different dimension of life. If only museums could capture the spirit of the man and not just a wax replica. Can we capture spirit through words? Through conversations? The wisdom of the past can come with us on the journey and not remained locked in a museum show room. By sharing flowers and our deeds of love and service we provide new facets of meaning.

JW Fairchild

*Kaitlyn mimics Abe Lincoln; Elizabeth under HUGE statue*

*Flowers for the Living*

This Flower is for: Don Fado

From: David Fado

JW Fairchild

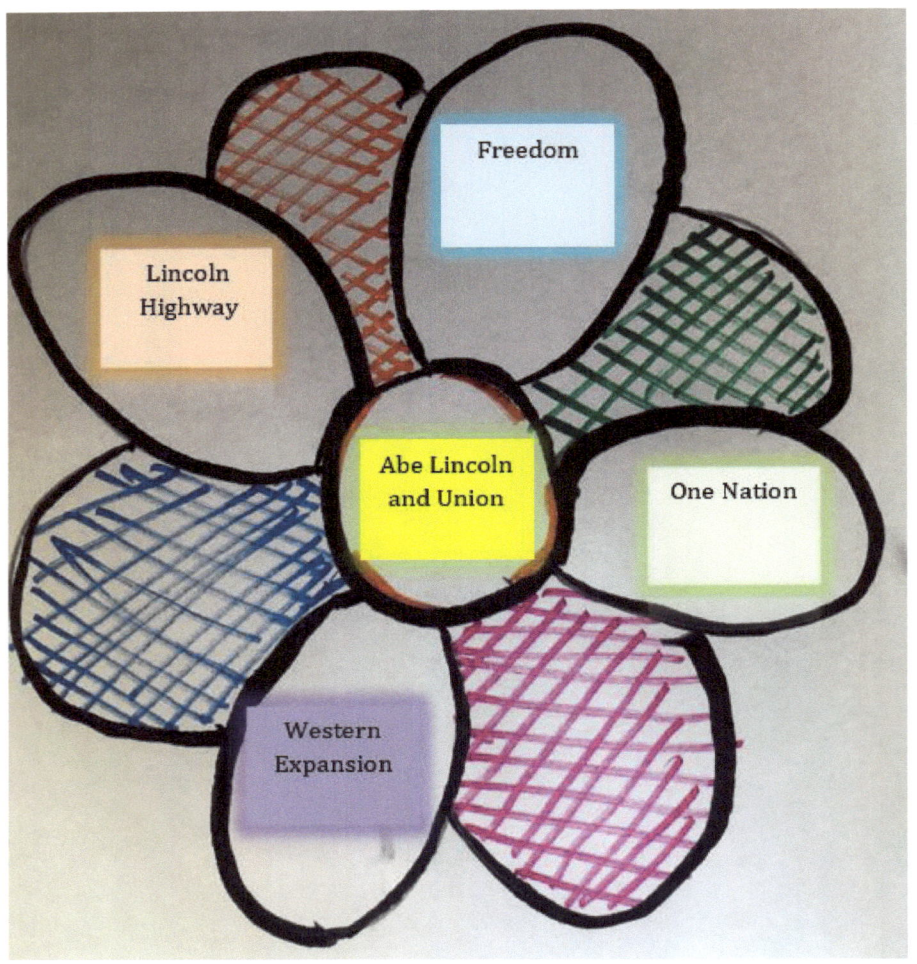

This Flower is for: Abraham Lincoln
From: David Fado

# Are You Old

## Original Text

In my boyhood days I thought when a man reached fifty he was an old man. That seemed to be the consensus of the people of that generation. But when I reached fifty I was still strong and active as when thirty, and others that age were so well preserved as I. So I had to move my age line up quite a bit. And at sixty I found people going strong and showing no scars from the scythe of Time.

A little research showed me that the Psalmist considered a man on the old list at seventy. He says, **"The days of our years are three score and ten; and if by reason of strength they be fourscore years, yet is their strength labor and sorrow." Psalm 90:10.**

As a rule no doubt the Psalmist was right. The majority of men and women show age at seventy, and after that point their failing strength labors in sorrow. But there are exceptions to rules, and I see men and women strong at fourscore. I know a man ninety-one who walks erect, uses no cane, and would be judged by appearance in his early seventies.

Your age is not measured by the number of years you have been upon earth, but by your attitude toward life. This is proved by the fact that people age much later than they used to.

When I was a boy, as soon as a girl married she pulled a bonnet down over her face, associated only with married people, and began to grow old. Her clothing, her associates, her entire attitude toward life presaged that age that was creeping upon her.

But now grandma dresses in clothes that a married girl of twenty would not have dared to wear sixty years ago (1895 as JW Fairchild wrote this in 1955). And she looks younger and feels younger than the granddaughters of those "good old days."

The prophet Joel gives us a standard by which to distinguish the young from the old. He says, **"Your old men shall dream dreams, your young shall see visions." Joel 2:28.**

Dreams are usually constructed from past experiences: visions are perceptions of things to take place in the future. Old men dream of the good old days gone by; the happy seasons they have had in the past, how good the people used to be, and what happy associations they had in the yesteryears. They live in the past, and feel that all that is worth living for is back in the bygone days.

But the young see visions. They grasp opportunities, see great achievements to be accomplished, and feel the best is still to come. They look forward, not backward.

And as long as man can see visions of work to be done, services to be rendered, plans to be carried out, purposes to be fulfilled, he is a young man, whether he is twenty or eighty.

But when a person begins to dream of the days gone by, and feel the best is in the past, and long for its return instead of working to make the future better than the past, he is old, whether he is twenty-five or seventy-five.

There is much in the saying that you are as old as you think you are. If you want to be old, retire, have nothing to do, not even a hobby to work at, but just sit around and let the world go by, and you will soon be in the class of the aged. But if you want to stay young, espouse some worthy cause, put your soul into it, associate with active people, take interest in the young, share their hopes and plans, and though your body will finally wear out, you will never grow old.

Are you old? In consecration and service you can "never grow old."

*Flowers for the Living*

Trails Notes 2: Age Quiz

Elizabeth was curious about my retyping activities and I decided to tell her about "Are You Old." I explained the point of the essay was the old were those who only dreamed of the past, while the young have visions of the future. She seemed curious, but unconvinced. Kaitlyn decided to come up with a quiz that one could take on an Ipad or at a restaurant waiting to eat. As she drew up the names of the contestants, she said she could predict the age just from the name. "No", I insisted, the point of the quiz was to determine whether a person is lost in dreams of the past or eager to implement visions in the future. I came up with this short quiz:

**Which do you like better: the new Mission Impossible series or the original? Put down the date.**

*My Answer: The new one, done in 2018.*

**List your three favorite Christmas memories then write down the year they occurred.**

*My Answer: The year I made cookies for Santa, 1971; the year with toy horses and Carolyn, 1996; and the year with the girl's castle, 2012.*

**Think of three things that make you smile and write them down. Then put the year.**

*My Answer: Don Fado spraying water from a flower, 2018; Elizabeth Fado throwing color guard flags, 2018; and Kaitlyn Fado making macaroons, 2018.*

**List your three favorite pets and the year they passed.**

*My answer: Mabel, dog, still alive; Tommy, cat, passed in 1982; and Sheba, dog passed in 1979.*

Tally up the years that have passed since your memories. This is an indicator of your age. I scored 152, so I am older, although I still love the passion of new visions. My girls scored much younger.

*Are U Old picture by Kaitlyn Fado*

"Your old men shall dream dreams, your young shall see visions." Joel 2:28.

# Soul Hunger

## Original Text

There are different kinds of hunger. Hunger for physical food is universal. Then some hunger for achievement, for wealth, for fame—for all the ambitions of life.

Besides these, there is a soul hunger, which worldly things cannot satisfy. It is an inward spiritual longing for something beyond the comprehension of our physical sense. You and I know what it means to feel there is something lacking; a vacancy within our hearts, which the things of time and sense can never fill. There is something wrong, but we don't know just what that wrong is.

So far as we know, this uneasiness, this restlessness, is not the result of any wrong we have done, or any duty left undone. It is not a condemnation, not common anxiety, dread, or fear, which at times assail all of us, but a hunger, a thirst, a soul longing which the treasures of earth cannot satisfy.

David calls this soul hunger a longing for God. **"My soul longeth, yea, even fainteth for the courts of the Lord: my heart and my flesh crieth out for the living God." Psalm 84:2.**

Think of it as you may, but there is a craving in our soul for spiritual food, and we can no more live spiritually without that food than we can live physically without material food.

Our heart and our flesh cry out for the living God, for the approbation of his spirit, assuring us all is well. We crave his presence, his companionship, his guiding spirit. And without that companionship, life to the child of God is a desolate wilderness, a journey alone through the deepness of the night.

His presence banishes every doubt, drives away every fear, and disperses every cloud. **"In his presence is fulness of joy, and at his right hand there are pleasures for evermore." Psalm 16:11.**

## JW Fairchild

We are very considerate about satisfying the hunger of those who need physical food. We would not knowingly let any one go hungry for food which we could supply. Among our neighbors, we would find few if any, who are suffering for bodily nourishment.

But if we could look into their hearts, see the struggles, the blasted hopes, the crushed ambitions, the longing for something beyond their reach, we would realize we are surrounded by more hungry souls than hungry stomachs—more people suffering from spiritual malnutrition than from physical malnutrition.

What are we doing about it? Are we trying to satisfy this soul hunger?

You ask, "what can we do to satisfy it?"

Remember that just a word, a smile, the clasp of the hand, often gives the strength and courage for that last weary smile.

*Flowers for the Living*

Trail Notes 3: Quilt for the Soul

Kaitlyn observed that Trail Trek 2018 visited cities and towns with obsessions. We anticipated Springfield's obsession for Abraham Lincoln, but we were not prepared for the quilt inspired town of Hamilton, Missouri. Labelled "Quilt Town, USA," Hamilton proved a remarkable find. This town had all things quilting. While early retailer JC Penney got his start in this area, today's quilting focused on training and techniques. What a wonderful collection of quilts.

While looking at quilting patterns and the beautiful samples I thought of JW's observation that **"we are surrounded by more hungry souls**

*Hamilton Missouri*

**than hungry stomachs—more people suffering from spiritual malnutrition than from physical malnutrition."** The quilts held my soul as only a warm blanket on a cold day can, stitching together themes of a life and family. The city had murals of quilts, which I used to guide the picture below. Another lesson learned from JW on the trip: look for ways to satisfy your soul hunger on the journey.

*2018 Quilt for the Soul*

# Change and the Changeless

## Original Text

Some people are very much opposed to change. They want things to continue just as they have in the past. But we live in a world of change. Seasons change, customs change, the mode of living changes, and if we do not adjust ourselves to changed conditions, we are doomed to perish. The dinosaurs, prehistoric animals, grew to be nearly one hundred feet long, and some of them weighed forty tons; but they all perished from the earth. Why did they become extinct? Climatic conditions changed, the means of life changed, but they did not change to meet the new situation, therefore, their doom was sealed.

Herein is a lesson for us. If we do not adapt ourselves to the new conditions under which we live, we too must perish. This is true of churches the same as of individuals. People's habits, customs, and mode of life are continually changing, and we must change with them or go the way of the dinosaurs.

But while customs, conditions, and modes of life are constantly changing, truth and principle never change. Two and two made four the day that God breathed into Adam's nostrils the breath of life and he became a living soul. Ages had passed before God shut Noah, his family and menagerie, in the ark, but two and two were still making four, and will continue to do so *ad infinitum.* No decree of king, act of parliament, or law passed by any legislative body can make two and two anything but four. That is a principle and can never be changed.

Inertia and gravitation were inherent in matter when the first orb was rolled out into space, and they perform their functions unerringly today. The centripetal and centrifugal forces held in their orbits the first planets that traveled through the heavens, and today the same forces keep harmony and order among the countless millions of stars and planets, and satellites, that grace the boundless expanse above us. These eternal laws of the universe never change.

And this is the reason that the religion of Jesus Christ is adaptable to every age, state and condition of the human race. It is founded upon principle, not on custom. It is adapted to the needs of the ignorant, the mediocre, and the educated alike. Great changes have taken place since Jesus preached the Sermon on the Mount, knowledge has been increased, and science has opened up new worlds of thought, but the truths set forth in that sermon meet our needs today the same as they did for those who heard the words fall from his lips. Had his teaching been based on custom or made to suit the special conditions of people at any given period, it would have gone with the Pharaohs, and passed into oblivion. But springing from truth and principles that are eternal and never change, the religion of Jesus Christ has always met the needs of those whose strength and wisdom were insufficient for the day, and will continue to do so as long as man continues to dwell on this terrestrial ball.

*Flowers for the Living*

Trail Notes 4: Elizabeth Fado, Great-Great-Granddaughter

Change is taken differently by everyone. Some are forcefully against any sort of change while others embrace it, maybe even forcing it into action. I myself believe that most people lay in between; in an existence where some or most changes that are inherently "good" or "bad" are rejected, feared, welcomed or appreciated.

When I was a child I hated abrupt changes. When I played with something I needed a warning to finish what I was doing before moving to another task so I would not raise a hissy fit. Now I understand that change is abrupt and inevitable and I am now more prepared than I was back then. I now understand that I need to be able to adapt to the changes, not run away from most of them.

My great-great-grandfather wrote about those who are not prepared for change to say they will not survive, his main example being dinosaurs. I don't disagree with him but I think that the dinosaurs really could not be prepared for a meteor, or whatever you believe happened to the dinosaurs.

I think a theme that I am supposed to follow is that of travel. My family recently went on an Oregon trail trip, consisting of us being in the car for about a week. Being in a car for about a week helps a lot with having time to reflect on yourself and humanity. The westward movement of the time was pushed by lots of powerful people in America and left the areas people traveled through irreversibly different than they were before. While on the trip I noticed that the westward movement was a very good thing for the Americans because it brought land and power, which countries love; just look back at why the British colonized America.

One argument could be made that the natives of the area were forced out of their land because they were "not prepared for change." This is where I find that ideology a bit dangerous. Saying that the reason why a group or a person did not survive or were cast aside is removing their possibly important narrative. I see what point his point was and see what he means but I feel like it is not the best explanation for why some don't survive. Change is inevitable and we should be prepared but not to the point of being paranoid without just reason. Change is inevitable and some things are changeless.

*Taco Bell in Iowa in August 2018 was not just closed, it was demolished. Change came to this location.*

# Predestination

Original Text

The noun predestination is not found in the Bible, but we are told that the verb "predestinate" is found four times–twice in **Romans 8:29, 30,** where it is translated **"predestinate,"** and twice in **Ephesians 1: 5, 11,** where it is translated **"predestinated,"** and that in every case it refers to salvation. From this many infer that predestination never refers to any thing not directly pertaining to the salvation of the Lord's people. But the Greek work *proorizo,* from which our word *"predestinate"* is translated, and found also in **1 Corinthians 2:7,** where it is translated **"ordained before"** and in **Acts 4:28**, where we have **"determined before."**

Wescott and Hort, noted Greek scholars, tell us that *proorizo* means "to predetermine," "to appoint beforehand," "to foreordain." This is in perfect harmony with the Latin *predestino,* which the Universal Dictionary defines, "to determine beforehand." If we accept these definitions, then the word, *"predestinate,"* simply means to determine beforehand; to decide what you intend to do before you do it. Before the farmer begins his crop, he decides what fields he will cultivate, and what kind of seed he will plant in each field. That is predestination. Before the architect begins the construction of a building, he draws his plans and specifications so complete that the workmen by following them erect the identical building which he had planned, or predestined to build. The completed house is only the blueprint materialized. That is predestination. Any one who decides before he does a thing what he is going to do, and how he is going to do it, uses predestination.

But look at it this way. If finite man would not build a house without deciding beforehand what kind of house he was going to build and the purpose that house was to serve, would the Infinite God, with whom are hid all the treasures of wisdom and knowledge, create a world with all that is in it, without deciding beforehand what kind of a world he was going to create and what purpose that world would fulfil? When God purposes a thing, determines that thing shall be done or come to pass, that is predestination. It matters not whether the purpose be the creation of a world, the sending of rain, the destruction of the wicked, or the salvation of the righteous. It is predestination just the same. So we might say predestination is an act of God, or man, by which he determines what he is going to do, have done, or suffer to be done, before it is done.

Is this definition clear? Do you see any flaw in it? If so, please point it out, and let's understand each other on what we mean by predestination. And now, if we are agreed on what predestination is, let us go a step further and consider what it embraces. Here is where the rub comes in. This is the point on which the main differences have hinged, and over which division has come.

When the architect draws his plans for a building what does he put in them? Does he not specify in the blueprint everything that goes into the building? If something is left out of the specifications, will it not also be left out of the building? And would not God, the All Wise Designer, make his designs as perfect and complete as fallible man makes his? If something is left out of the design would it not also be left out in the execution? So all that is must have been purposed, designed, predestinated, or the design was incomplete.

In this discussion it is not necessary for us to prove that God predestinated the good deeds of men, for no one objects to that. Many of our people claim God has not predestinated the wicked deeds of men. And the main reason for opposing the teaching that God had predestinated the wicked deeds of men is that they claim it would make him the author of sin.

Well I would oppose any doctrine that charges sin to God. Sin is contrary to the very nature of God. God is essentially good, and can no more do or authorize that which is evil than a good tree can bear corrupt fruit. God never causes, tempts, or influences any one to sin.

*Flowers for the Living*

**"Let no man say when he is tempted, I am tempted of God: for God cannot be tempted with evil, neither tempteth he any man." James 1:13.** God hates sin, condemns sin, punishes sin, but never tempts or influences man to sin. Sin springs not from God, but from man. **"Every man is tempted when he is drawn away with his own lusts and enticed." James 1:14.** It is our lustful nature that draws us into sin, and no one has a right to charge his sin to God's predestination.

Predestination is not the incentive or motive power that causes men to do either good or bad deeds. Men do good deeds, not because it was predestinated they should do them, but because they are prompted by a righteous spirit to do them. And they do evil deeds, not because it was predestinated they should do them, but because they are moved by an evil spirit to do them. Men do good deeds for the same reason that a good tree bears good fruit, and evil deeds for the same reason a corrupt tree bears corrupt fruit.

Is not that clear? The thing you have to understand is that there is a vast difference between God's predestinating a thing and authorizing or causing that thing to come to pass. The Bible clearly teaches that God has predestinated many of the wicked deeds of men, but it as clearly teaches that God does not cause, authorize, or influence men to do any of those wicked deeds. No more wicked deed was ever committed by men or devils than the betrayal, condemnation and crucifixion of Jesus Christ. Any yet his inspired servants tell us, **"For of a truth against thy holy child Jesus whom thou hast anointed, both Herod and Pontius Pilate, with the Gentiles and the people of Israel, were gathered together, for to do WHATSOEVER THY HAND AND THY COUNSEL DETERMINED BEFORE TO BE DONE." Acts, 4: 27, 28.** The whole mob, Jews, Gentiles, Herod, Pontius Pilate, doing whatsoever the hand and counsel of God determined before to be done. "Before determine" and predestinated come from the same Greek word, *proorizo,* so those who betrayed, condemned and crucified the Savior did just what God had predestinated they should do.

But while God predestinated that this should be done, was he the author of those men's sins? Did he cause or influence them to do it? Certainly not. Listen to the Apostle Peter: **"Him being delivered by the determinate counsel and foreknowledge of God, ye have taken, and with wicked hands have crucified and slain."** Acts 2: 23.

God not only foreknew, but also before determined that they should condemn and crucify Jesus, and yet they did it with "wicked hands." They knew nothing about God's purpose in the death of Jesus, and voluntarily condemned and put him to death. They were just as guilty as they would have been if God had not "before determined" or predestinated it. They knew him not, nor understood the voice of the prophets which they read, and **"fulfilled them in crucifying him."** Acts 13: 27.

Will anyone claim that these men were not responsible for their deeds because they fulfilled God's purpose? No, they did it "with wicked hands."

No doubt some one will want to know how God can predestinate an act and not be the cause or author of it. I have already shown that predestination is not the force that causes men to act, but as this is the crux of the question, let me further illustrate. Over in Eastern Tennessee there are many large springs—good size streams springing out of the earth and wending their way toward the sea. They run through rich narrow valleys, and often cut away the banks and carry off the soil. If left to take their course they would wash away much of the soil, but those farmers save much of their soil by keeping the stream in proper bounds. They will cut a new channel and straighten the stream in one place, and put in an abutment to protect the bank in another. They do not cause the water to flow down stream, but they do determine its channel and thus save their land.

## *Flowers for the Living*

Sometimes those farmers go further than just preventing the stream from washing away their land. They will direct it in an entirely new channel, create a current for it, and bring it around the side of the mountain to where it will have a great fall. Here they build a mill and use the force of the water in its fall to run the machinery. They did not cause the water to flow down stream, but they fixed its channel, directed its course, utilized its power and not only prevented it from destroying their lands, but made it grind their wheat and corn, and in many other ways serve the community. Who will say those farmers did wrong in fixing the channel of the stream and turning it into a blessing instead of leaving it to take its course and wash away their best soil?

God no more causes men to do wickedly than those Tennessee farmers caused the water to flow down the stream. The water runs down stream because the force of gravity draws it that way; and men do wickedly because their evil lustful nature draws them that way. And as men fix the channel of the stream and turn the force of the water into a blessing, so God sets the bounds of the wicked, lays out the path they shall travel, determines or predestinates what things they may do and what things they shall not do, and thus confines their wickedness in such a channel that it works for the good of them that love God. That is not bad of God, is it? Aren't you glad God has fixed the bounds of the wicked? If the wicked were turned loose, unrestricted and unbounded by God's decree, where would our safety be? I am not so much concerned as to whether he has determined or predestinated the wicked acts of men. Only by the bounds of the wicked being unalterably set can the righteous be secure.

Aren't we agreed on this? At this point our limited and unlimited predestinarians can find a common meeting ground. The contention of our limited brethren that God is not the author of sin and in no sense tempts men to sin, is not only granted but advocated as strongly as they advocate it. And our unlimited brethren's argument that God's predestination or determinate counsel extends to all the wicked actions of men and devils, fixing their bounds, governing their deeds, determining what they may do and they may not, is set forth in perfect harmony with his goodness and perfection. Does not each here find all for which he is contending, and nothing contrary to it?

I have already shown that predestination is NEVER CAUSATIVE. Regarding predestination as causative is at the bottom of most of the trouble over the question. There is a vast difference in God's attitude toward righteousness and his attitude toward sin. He approves the one and condemns the other; influences men to do the one and punishes them for doing the other. But predestination is only *determinative*, and God determines the acts of the wicked in the same way that he determines the acts of the righteous. He may predestinate to cause a good deed to be done, or to suffer an evil one to be done, but predestination is only the decision in the matter and not the cause of permission. The difference in God's predestination of the good and evil acts of men is not a difference in kinds or predestination, but a difference in the things predestinated. There is no such thing as a causative or permissive predestination, but God does predestinate to cause some things to be done and to permit others to be done.

If predestination were causative, all that a man would have to do to realize his desires would be to determine or decide in his mind (predestinate) just what he wants. Then the predestination would cause those things to come to him. But let the architect stop when his blueprint is finished and see if his building will go up. Workmen must put into execution that which the designer has planned or predestinated, or not even the foundation will be laid.

One of the great difficulties in understanding predestination is that most people overlook the fact that God governs the universe according to law. The reign of law is supreme, and nothing transpires outside of it from the whirring of a gnat's wings to the movements of the heavenly bodies. Even the thoughts of our minds are as subject to law as the freezing and thawing of ice.

## Flowers for the Living

Yet you may ask: If this be true, where does God come in? If the universe is governed by law what does God have to do with it? Does not the reign of law supersede his control and leave him out of the arrangement? No. The universe is not governed BY law, but it is governed by the Lord, ACCORDING TO law. Universal law is God's way of doing things, so the reign of law but carries out God's predestination—brings to pass the things which he has predestinated or determined shall come to pass.

Here let us consider the difference between what we may call a mechanical predestination and one in harmony with universal law. According to mechanical predestination God would send us rain by pulling the stoppers out of the clouds and letting the water pour out, and then stop the rain by sticking the stoppers back into the clouds. But true predestination, predestination according to law, gives us rain by proper atmospheric conditions prevailing.

Let me further illustrate. You have probably met people who would tell you that God had predestinated that a certain apple should fall from a certain twig at a certain second, and that it cannot fall a second sooner nor hold on a second longer. You thought you did not believe it, but that is just what you and I do believe. Of course we do not believe that when that second arrives God literally knocks the apple off the tree. There are two forces or laws that govern the fall of that apple. One is cohesion, which binds it to the twig; the other is gravity, which pulls it toward the earth; and the very second when gravity becomes stronger than cohesion that apple will fall and not until then. Of course other forces might augment the force of gravity and cause the apple to fall sooner than if left for gravity alone to pull it off. If the wind should blow that would add to the force of gravity and it might make the apple fall sooner, but in that case the force of the wind would be put into the calculation and the apple would fall at the appointed time.

Here is a good place to consider that age old question, "Is there a fixed time for man to die, and he can't die before that time, nor live a moment longer after it does come?" I have heard this question discussed ever since I can remember; one side contending that the day is unalterably fixed, the other that it is not fixed at all. Let us impartially consider it for a moment.

The patriarch Job answered this question, when in speaking of man, he said, **"Seeing his days are determined, the number of his months are with thee, thou hast appointed his bounds that he cannot pass." Job 14: 5.** If man's days are determined (predestinated), if the number of his months is with the Lord, and his bounds are appointed so that he cannot pass them, when his time is up don't you think he will have to shuffle off?

But someone is ready to ask, "Don't you think a man may lengthen or shorten his days?"

Yes sir, I think if a man is standing on a railroad track in front of a moving train it is pretty certain he will live longer if he gets off the track than he would if he remains on it and lets the train run over him. There are thousands of people alive today who would been in their graves had it not been for medical treatment or a surgical operation. We have often heard it said that a physician can ease pain, but he cannot save life. If a man is bleeding to death and a physician ties the artery or vein and stops the blood, has he not saved the man's life? If a person is drowning and another rescues him, he certainly saves his life, and the man lives longer than he would if left to drown. Hezikiah's life was lengthened fifteen years by binding a fig poultice on a boil. And barring accidents we shall all live longer if we obey the laws of health than we would if we disobey them.

This in no sense contradicts the idea that the date of a man's death is fixed, but it does show that if the end of his life is set, all things else that have a bearing on his life must be so fixed to bring him to that hour, and the means must be there to take him away. It was as surely predestinated that the poultice should be applied to Hezekiah's boil, as it was that his days should be prolonged fifteen years. There is no more inconsistent teaching than that the date of a man's death is fixed,

## Flowers for the Living

but the other things have a bearing on his life are left to chance. Suppose it is predestinated that you shall die on the 24th day of April 1956. You can't die before that time, and you can't live longer. But some tell us the acts of the wicked are not predestinated or fixed. If not, there is nothing to prevent a murderer from shooting you through the heart tomorrow. Your heart torn apart until it can no longer pump the blood through your body you cannot live, but because your time has not come you cannot die. Wouldn't you be in a fix? Does not this show clearly that if the date of your death is fixed or predestinated, the acts of yourself and others much be so fixed as to permit you to live till that appointed time? If this be true, then if a thing is predestinated all other things preceding it in the line of cause and effect must also be fixed to insure that thing's coming to pass. From this premise you may draw your own conclusion as to what things must be included in predestination.

JW Fairchild

## Trail Notes 5: Maps of a Planned Trip

For Trail Trek, we saw many maps that charted the journeys and challenges of the pioneers. In such a land, a father would know the need to plan the journey, respect the rules of nature, and not leave all to God's predetermination. Along the way, those rules and the word of God shaped the journey into clear "predestined" steps, or markers. On the giant painted map of westward expansion below are the pictures of predestined markers.

The journey starts with Independence. The pioneers who moved west all knew the risks and challenges in front of them: their own skill and talent would determine whether they reached the goals. As we followed the trail, we saw the signs of community everywhere, from Fort Kearney on to the wagon trains. Across the great plains, the grandeur of the world God created bursts through, from Chimney Rock to the continental divide.

*A journey*

## Flowers for the Living

We took the California, or Donner trail, in part to visit friends in Salt Lake City and also because we had a place to stay in Lake Tahoe. In Independence, Elizabeth and Kaitlyn grew curious about the Donner Party. Kaitlyn got a shirt that said "Hungry for Change? Vote for the Donner Party" that she wore. I knew in general the horrors that party went through to survive winter, but it would take this trip to fully appreciate the struggle across the trail.

JW Fairchild's fixation on predestination made sense when faced with raw wilderness. Previously my interest in predestination did not go far past the Rush verse, "I will choose free will." I do not believe God predestined the outcome of every action nor do I believe that God takes away my responsibility to make smart decisions. My father never taught me to avoid taking responsibility, nor did my grandfather. Although my great-grandfather argued for predestination in the primitive Baptist community, he did not see predestination as a script with no free will. God put in place the pattern of a journey.

None of this will happen with just talking: action is required. As JW writes, **"let the architect stop when his blueprint is finished and see if his building will go up. Workmen must put into execution that which the designer has planned or predestinated, or not even the foundation will be laid."** For JW and his family, that foundation is built from independence, community, the rules of nature, the Word of God and the struggle to overcome barriers. With those foundations, the family and community has the tools to reach their goals.

As a family that has benefited from what JW built, I am thankful he put in place such a strong foundation.

**Marks and signed rocks at the start of the Oregon Trail**

# Struggle—The Price of Victory

## Original Text

Struggle is the law of growth. No plant, no animal, no individual or organization ever grew to maturity without struggle. And "the harder the fight the greater the victory," is true in plant and animal development, and in human achievement, as well as in the decisive battles of war.

When one people have oppressed another people they have always done so at their own peril. In the long run, the oppressors are the losers, and the oppressed the gainers. In Egypt, when a king arose who knew not Joseph, and made the Israelites serve with rigor, he sealed his own doom, and made way for the freedom of the children of Israel. By his own cruelty and hardness of heart, he brought ruin and destruction to his own country, death to himself, and sent the Hebrews on their way to the Promised Land.

One reason for the laxity and indifference among church people today is the lack of opposition. The so-called Christian life is one of comparative ease. It holds out no challenge to grapple with danger. The stake, the gibbet, and the dungeon no longer try their faith. While I hope those tortures never again make martyrs of saints, the path of ease and pleasure has never appealed to men and women of zeal and courage. The spirit of humanity is dulled with ease, but never quenched by trials and afflictions.

When people worshipped God at their own peril, when public prayer exposed them to the lion's den, and refusal to bow down to images set up by kings meant the fiery furnace, they were far more loyal to their Master than they are in this day of ease and approval.

The Mormon church would probably be little known today had it not been for the persecution and affliction which they had to endure. But to them, persecution was a challenge, and afflictions a spur, that put determination and zeal into them, so that they turned a desert into a fertile field, erected templates that stand as monuments to their skill and industry, and engrave their names indelible on the pages of history.

I am not advocating nor endorsing the Mormon religion, but using this illustration to show that in them it is demonstrated that struggle is the law of growth.

*Flowers for the Living*

## Trail Notes 6: Out of Struggle, Beauty in Utah

The trip down the mountains from Wyoming into Utah and Salt Lake City scared the heck out of the family in a minivan; I can't imagine the trip in a covered wagon into such a harsh environment. It must have felt like sliding into hell. To this day, the people of the west have responded to afflictions as a spur to improve and make life better. Salt Lake City is a remarkable wonder.

Still, just beyond the lakes we crossed the sea of salt that so challenged the Donner Party. After a few hours in the car driving through the salt, I wondered again how one could walk this trail for days.

**Utah Salt Flats**

# Robbing God

## Original Text

In the church of which I am a member, if a man will not pay his debts he is excommunicated. Members must not only wash their feet, but also pay their debts and tell the truth. And if a member was caught robbing his fellowman, his name would immediately be crossed off the church record.

True religion puts honesty into the hearts of men and women. The grace of God will make a liar tell the truth, an extortioner help the needy, and a thief to steal no more. It will transform a desperado into a law-abiding citizen, and turn an alcoholic into a sober man. It is the only hope of the redemption of the world from crime and corruption.

While robbing men is strictly taboo in our church, one may rob God with impunity, so far as the church is concerned. But is it a greater crime to rob men than it is to rob God? Is it worse to fail to pay your debt to man than to God?

In the third chapter of the Book of Malachi, we read, **"Will a man rob God? Yet ye have robbed me. But ye say, Wherein have we robbed thee? In tithes and in offerings. Ye are cursed with a curse: for ye have robbed me, even this whole nation."**

Then the Lord challenges Israel to **"Bring ye all the tithes into the storehouse, that there may be meat in mine house, and prove me now herewith, saith the Lord of hosts, if I will not open you the windows of heaven, and pour you out a blessing, that there shall not be room enough to receive it." Malachi 3:8-10.**

Under the Mosaic law, Israelites were required to pay tithes, and when they failed to pay them, they robbed God. In the New Testament we find no such command. The idea that one-tenth of what we possess belongs to God is only part truth. All we possess is God's.

We are his stewards, to use what he has entrusted to us as he directs, and when we fail to give according to his demands, we rob God.

The first church at Jerusalem did not tithe. They gave all they possessed. They were one-hundred percenters, not tithers. They did not rob God, and as a result, **"Great grace was upon them all. Neither was there any among them that lacked…." Acts 4:33-34.** But Ananias and Sapphira did rob God, and lost their lives as a consequence. And many of God's people are losing their lives spiritually today, for the same reason.

We are under obligation to support God's kingdom, and when we fail to give according as he has prospered us, we rob God. We are blessed in obedience, and punished in disobedience today, as they were under the law of Moses.

We must therefore fulfill our voluntary obligations even though tithing is not commanded in the New Testament.

*Flowers for the Living*

## Trail Notes 7: The Great Gifts of Creation

As the trail continued, we sped across Nevada and into Reno. The kids suddenly got very excited. Were they happy to see trees? No. They saw a Del Taco sign that said "fresh avocado." They shouted "where is the free 'sha voca do.'" I had no idea what this meant. Later I learned about the meme of a customer demanding their "free sha voca do" based on a misreading of a Del Taco sign like that pictured below. What engages someone's perspective after a trek of a thousand miles can be hard to predict. I imagine what captivated the Donner Party were the green trees and lakes as they moved in the Tahoe region. That said, a fast food restaurant might have captivated them more: the Donner Party lacked "free sha voca do" or any fast food.

*Where is my FREE Sha Voca Do?*

For us, after some fresh avocado, we rolled into Lake Tahoe and it looked like paradise. Some beauty is easier to appreciate on a full stomach.

JW Fairchild

*Lake Tahoe*

# Happiness

## Original Text

Happiness is the state of being satisfied with your situation; of having a contented mind, and enjoying the things you are doing. It is what all men and women desire, and the thing most of them are seeking.

Epicurus, a Greek philosopher, who taught in Athens some 300 years before Christ, taught that pleasure is the only good; and to gratify the senses and satisfy the appetite should be the purpose of life. Whatever gives pleasure is good; what is unpleasant is bad. The Epicureans are numerous today, in life, if not in name.

This extreme view was a reaction against the austere doctrine of the Cynics, who taught that all pleasure is sinful, and to be happy is to indulge in the lusts of the flesh. They lived on the coarsest of food, and sought to mortify all desire. There were many teachers of Cynicism, but the most famous of them was Diogenes, who practically starved himself, and it is said he slept in a tub.

Both these positions are extreme, and neither conducive to true happiness. Righteousness, and not pleasure, should be the purpose of life: but there can be no harm in pleasure which harms neither yourself nor anyone else. Anything that injures yourself, or anyone else, physically, mentally, morally or spiritually, is sin. It is a sin to injure these bodies which God has given us to serve Him and humanity in, and when we do so we cannot be happy. All habits, which violate the laws of nature, and bring pain and distress, are destructive to happiness.

Some think the way to be happy is to have an abundance of this world's goods. How many people think they will be happy when they get a home, a car, or some other coveted possession! But when they get them, there are other things they want as much as these, and are not happy until they get them. But happiness can never come by accumulating things, for the more you acquire the more you want.

**"He that loveth silver shall not be satisfied with silver; nor he that loveth abundance with increase." Ecclesiastes 5:10.** Happiness comes from within, not from without. And if there is sunshine in the soul, storms without cannot destroy its happiness.

It is our duty to be happy. The happy person scatters sunshine along the path of others, banishes their fears, drives away their doubts, and gives them courage for the road. What is more inspiring and encouraging than to associate with a happy person? It is like coming into the sunshine out of the darkness and gloom; or sitting in the shade when the heat is scorching. But to dwell with a grouchy despondent person is like having icy water thrown on your body. It drives happiness away, and covers your sky with murky clouds.

Happiness can never be attained by seeking it. Those who seek happiness for happiness' sake get pricked by the thorn instead of plucking the rose. Happiness springs from sacrifice, not from indulgence. It is always bound up in service to others. Self-satisfaction brings regret and remorse, but sacrifice for others fills the soul with joy, and brings true happiness.

There is no happiness equal to victory won. But victory lost through self-indulgence, through yielding to the pleasure of the senses, destroys all happiness and makes you abhor yourself. Victory won, no matter how hard the fight, how much pain and suffering you must endure to win it, always fills the soul with happiness.

So the way to be happy is to conquer self; to overcome habits that are injurious; to renounce the world, the flesh, and the devil; and give your life in service to God and humanity.

David expressed the state of true happiness when he said, **"A day in the courts is better than a thousand. I had rather be a doorkeeper in the house of my God than to dwell in the tents of wickedness." Psalm 84:10.** To have God's presence with you, to feel the approval of his spirit within you, to have a conscience void of offence toward God and man, to help the weak, to console the sorrowful, to comfort

## Flowers for the Living

those in distress, and bind up broken hears, make life worth living, and fill our days with HAPPINESS.

JW Fairchild

## Trail Notes 8: Carolyn Fado, Great-Great-Granddaughter

**Where is this child?**
By Carolyn Fado

*Where is she—*

*that child at Xmas*
*filled with bliss?*
*Remember*
*her presence by the presents,*
*how she lit up the tree*
*and filled the room with glee?*

*Where is she—*
*that girl*
*who ran to play*
*that first December*
*snow-day,*
*skipping - sledding,*
*creating*
*snow-angels,*
*her back*
*in the snow?*

*Where did she go?*

*She's*
*no longer wild, she's*
*calm and mild, she's*
*still with a smile,*
*a smile so still it's*
*a willed and plastered*
*mask, ready for*
*the moment they*
*ask her,*
*"How are you?"*

*Flowers for the Living*

"I'm fine, and you?"
If only words could
make it true.

We live a life of
liberty and the pursuit
of happiness.
This adult pursuit's no longer cute;
her emotions on mute,
her job robs her of her joy,
but she'll buy a grown-up toy,
and could it bring her joy?

With her health and wealth,
what else? What else
could a person need?

What else? What else
could a person need
to just succeed?

Before your
soul's bought out by greed,
take heed,
take heed.
Help someone in need.

Before your
soul's bought out by greed,
take heed,
take heed.
Help someone in need.

JW Fairchild

*Mabel, age one, eagerly awaits gifts from Carolyn! She needs lots of love and affection.*

# "But if Not"

## Original Text

Nebuchadnezzar, king of Babylon, made an image of gold, which was 90 feet high and nine feet wide, and set it up in the plain of Dura, in the province of Babylon. Then Nebuchadnezzar gathered together the princes, governors, and all the rulers of Babylon, to come to the dedication of the image which he had set up. They came and stood before the image.

Then a herald proclaimed: **"To you it is commanded, O peoples, nations and languages, that at what time ye hear the sound of the cornet, flute, harp, sackbut, psaltery, dulcimer, and all kinds of music, ye fall down and worship the golden image that Nebuchadnezzar the king hath set up: and whoso falleth not down and worshippeth shall the same hour be cast into the midst of a burning fiery furnace." Daniel 3:4-6.**

The people fell down and worshipped. But three Jews in captivity who had gained favor with the king, who made them officers in Babylon: Shadrach, Meshach and Abednego, were loyal to their God, and did not fall down and worship the golden image.

Some Chaldeans told the king of these Jews who refused to obey his orders, and informed him that they do not obey his gods, nor worship the image which he had set up. Nebuchadnezzar was very angry, and commanded that Shadrach, Meshach and Abednego be brought to him. When they were brought to the king, he asked them, "Is it true that you do not serve my gods, nor worship the golden image which I have set up?" But the king was rather liberal, and offered to give them another chance. That if they would be ready when they heard the sound of music, and fall down and worship the image, all would be well; but if they did not worship the golden image, they would be cast the same day into the midst of the burning fiery furnace.

Shadrach, Meshach and Abednego said to the king: **"O Nebuchadnezzar, we are not careful to answer thee in this matter. If it be so, our God whom we serve is able to deliver us from the burning fiery furnace, and he will deliver us out of thine hand, O king. BUT IF NOT, be it known unto thee, O king, that we will not serve thy gods, nor worship the golden image which thou hast set up." Daniel 3:16-18.**

It is easy enough to be loyal and true to our God when we have the assurance that he will take care of us. **"BUT IF NOT,"** on the assumption that God will not intervene and save us from the fiery furnace. While three persons were saved from the flames of the furnace, thousands of as loyal souls have perished at the stake. While Daniel was protected from the mouths of the lions, thousands have been torn and mangled and slaughtered by lions in the arena at Rome. God can always deliver if it be his will, **"but if not,"** we should be as faithful and true as if deliverance were assured.

God has not promised to keep us out of trouble, but to be with us in our troubles. He did not keep the three Hebrew children out of the fiery furnace, but was with them in it. He did not keep Daniel out of the den of lions, but he was with him and locked the jaws of the lions so they could do no harm. He does not save us from all our sorrow, suffering and distress, but he makes these afflictions work together for our good.

Today no longer does the den of lions await us who worship and serve God rather than man and his idols. But we often meet situations in which self-interest conflicts with duty; in which loyalty to God means suffering and apparent loss to self. What is our course then?

God could protect us from all danger and shield us from all harm, and he does when it is his will. **"But if not,"** if he leaves us to suffer and perish in the flames, are we loyal then? God knows best, does all for the best, and all our suffering and distress are for our good. So let us do God's will, leave the consequences with him, and if it is ours to perish in the conflict, let us know that such light affliction, which is

*Flowers for the Living*

but for a moment, worketh for us a far more exceeding and eternal weight of glory.

JW Fairchild

## Trail Notes 9: Donna Fado Ivery, Great-Granddaughter

Donna Fado Ivery, my sister and great-granddaughter of JW Fairchild, is a minister. She spent eight years working with editors and coaches to complete her book, *Sleep, Pray, Heal: A Path to Wholeness and Well-Being*. Donna's message provides a current illustration of JW Fairchild's observation that **"God has not promised to keep us out of trouble, but to be with us in our troubles."** Below is a summary of what led Donna to write her book, in her own words.

I'm a mother, wife, artist, and a United Methodist minister of thirty-plus years. What I'm really known for is my story. Twenty-five years ago, in January 1994, a two-hundred pound glass partition fell on my head resulting in brain injury, disability, and chronic pain. For seventeen years I relied on opiates, a cane, and sometimes a wheelchair to get around.

Now I walk freely.

I bring a unique perspective and expertise to the healing journey. With my words awash, I painted my prayers and God answered in the paintings. Brain injury graced me with having to rely on the Holy Spirit in new ways. Sharing the good news of spirituality and the way that God makes a way out of no way is my calling.

Although I am no longer able to pastor full-time, I have shared my story as preacher, keynote speaker, and teacher across the US. Especially caregivers and those who endure long-term suffering tell me that they have found hope and solace in my message. They have encouraged me to press on and write a book.

After a successful crowd-funding campaign, *Sleep, Pray Heal: A Path to Wholeness and Well-Being*, is now available for purchase from www.DonnaFadoIvery.com.

# A Little Bit of Honey

## Original Text

When famine gripped the land of Canaan in its clutches, Jacob sent ten of his sons to Egypt, where there was plenty of grain, to buy food. On their arrival in Egypt, the ruler of the land spoke roughly to them, accused them of coming to spy out the land, and by questions learned that their father was still living, and that their youngest brother, Benjamin, was at home with his father. He let them return with their grain, but told them they could see his face no more until they brought their brother Benjamin, to prove that their words were true. And he kept Simeon as a hostage till Benjamin should be brought.

When they returned home and made their report, Jacob was much upset, and refused to let Benjamin go with them to Egypt. Not knowing that Joseph was ruler in the land of Egypt, but thinking him dead, Jacob said, **"My son shall not go down with you; for his brother is dead, and he is left alone, if mischief befall him in the way in which ye go, then shall ye bring down my gray hairs with sorrow to the grave." Genesis 42:38.**

But hunger is more persuasive than words; and when their food was consumed, and Jacob was convinced that the only way to get more was to permit Benjamin to be taken along with the other boys on their next trip to Egypt, he consented.

Jacob told his boys to take a gift to the ruler of the land, and in that gift include **"a little bit of honey."** They thought they had to deal with a cruel, rough man; and when dealing with a self-willed, determined man it is always wise to give him a little bit of honey. You can't overcome opposition with bitter words. Honey is better than gall in winning an adversary. You can't catch flies with vinegar nor calm rage with bitterness of spirit. But **"a little bit of honey"** can do both.

**"Pleasant words are as a honeycomb, sweet to the soul, and health to the bones." Proverbs 16:24.** A little bit of honey, distributed in a few pleasant words, can allay opposition, subdue resentment, put the mind in a receptive mood, and bring peace and agreement to alienated hearts. **"A soft answer turneth away wrath, but grievous words stir up anger." Proverbs 15:1.** So in trying to win an adversary, always give a soft answer, speak pleasant words, use **"a little bit of honey."**

Nothing can soothe the weary soul, and calm the troubled mind, like gentle words, soft answers, and a sympathetic attitude. A little bit of praise will strengthen the bonds of affection and drive doubt from the wondering mind. But praise, like honey, should be used in moderation.

Those who have tried it know that Solomon was right when he said, **"It is not good to eat much honey." Proverbs 25:27.** Probably it takes as little honey to make one sick as anything one could eat. **"Hast thou found honey? Eat as much as is sufficient for thee, lest thou be filled therewith and vomit it." Proverbs 25:16.**

Sometimes we use too much honey; we exaggerate with our pleasant words of praise; they become flattery, and disgust the one we seek to please. Jacob sent only **"a little bit of honey"** to the ruler of Egypt; Jonathan tasted **"a little bit of honey"** when pursuing the enemy, and his eyes were enlightened and his strength renewed.

It takes less honey than almost any other food to satisfy the appetite. A little bit of honey goes a long way. Also, a few pleasant words, some little deeds of love and affection, give strength and courage to the faint, and save them from giving up the fight and falling by the way. It is little things in life that count for most. One man in a thousand may perform some great heroic deed once in a lifetime that brings him honor and fame, but such marvelous deeds usually affect but few.

It is little words of kindness, the little deeds of love and mercy, bestowed day by day upon those with whom we come in contact, that

## Flowers for the Living

lighten the loads of the many, bring joy and gladness into their hearts, and make life for them worth living.

**"A little bit of honey"** may accomplish more than a barrel of soup.

JW Fairchild

## Trail Notes 10: Humor Keeps the Edge

As a boy, my father Don Fado loved radio shows. Before he decided to dedicate his life to the gospel, a career in speech and radio comedy called to him. He took his love of humor and comedy and wove those threads into his sermons. His best sermons move from incredible laughter to profound passion.

JW Fairchild also understood how to weave multiple thoughts and insights into a tapestry. I read "A Little Bit of Honey" as we reached the end of the trip in Sacramento, where Don Fado currently lives. I was struck that just like my father, JW did not want to indulge any one emotion or theme at the exclusion of seeing the whole picture.

The family visited old town Sacramento, to see iron horses and towns that replaced the horses and covered wagons of the pioneers. Dad also provided a flower for me and his granddaughters in old town Sacramento: at the end of the trail, the flowers gave us the water!

*Don Fado with squirting flower*

# Why Serve God

## Original Text

The above question does not mean to infer that it might be unnecessary to serve God, but I am asking you the reason for the service which you are rendering. What is the motive, or incentive, which moves you to that service? The motive backing your deeds determines the quality of those deeds.

One of the basic reasons given as to why we should serve the Lord is that it pays to do so. That those who serve God are blessed in this life, and will finally enjoy heaven and immortal glory. Therefore if you are rendering the service in order to get those blessings, you are serving self instead of God. If your purpose in obeying God is to obtain a blessing, your service is selfish. You are not denying yourself for Jesus' sake, but seeking your own aggrandizement in Jesus' name. Service to God must contain sacrifice and self-denial, but never the hope of reward.

But you ask, "Does it not pay to serve God?" Indeed it does. Nothing in life yields as great dividends as service to God. But while it pays to serve God, *you cannot serve God for pay*. If the pay is what you are seeking, it is not God, but the pay, that you love. Jesus said, **"But seek ye first the kingdom of God and his righteousness; and all these things shall be added unto you."** Matthew 6:33.

By experience you probably know that is true. Those who put God's kingdom and righteousness first shall have their needs supplied. But suppose you should say in your heart, "I would certainly like to have food, clothing, and drink. Jesus has promised to give them to me if I will seek his kingdom and righteousness first. That is an offer I can't afford to turn down. I am going to seek them and make sure I have these necessary things added." Do you think you would receive them under such conditions? The fact is you would not be seeking God's kingdom and righteousness at all. You would be seeking those temporal things, and trying to get them through deception. You would be serving self in Jesus' name.

Neither the hope of reward nor the fear of punishment has ever influenced anyone to serve the Lord. As already shown, the hope of reward puts self-interest before God; and the fear of punishment does the same. If you are obeying God's commands in order to escape punishment, you are trying to save your own hide, and have no interest in God except to use him for your own advantage.

The three Hebrew children were not looking for a reward, nor seeking to save themselves from punishment, when they braved the fiery furnace. All they desired was to be loyal to God and do his will. The same was true with Daniel when he spent the night with the lions in their den. In each case it looked like destruction instead of deliverance, but they were not considering their own welfare. The loyal servant of God serves him whether it brings joy or sorrow, ease or pain, a cross or a crown, life or death. He follows in the footsteps of his Master, whether they lead in green pastures and beside still waters, or across burning, desert sands, over cold barren mountains, or through floods and flames. The stake, the gibbet, and the executioner's block cannot turn him from the path of duty, because he is drawn by God's love, which is stronger than death. Like the apostle Paul, they are ready not to be bound only, but also to die for the name of Jesus Christ, not counting their own lives dear to themselves, that they might finish their course with joy.

Love is the only motive which prompts any one to serve God, because love **"seeketh not her own." 1 Corinthians 13:5.** Love always makes us put the one we love before ourselves; and when we love God, we gladly deny ourselves that his will may be done in us. May this love bind us to God and keep us loyal to him like our fathers who had **"trial of cruel mocking and scourgings, yea, moreover of bonds and imprisonments. They were stoned, they were sawn asunder, were tempted, were slain with the sword; they wandered about in sheepskins and goat skins; being destitute, afflicted,**

*Flowers for the Living*

**tormented." Hebrews 11:36-37.** They were neither seeking a reward, nor trying to escape punishment, but doing the will of the one they loved.

*"Faith of our fathers, living still,*
*In spite of dungeon, fire and sword;*
*Oh how our hearts beat high with joy,*
*Whene'er we hear that glorious word.*
*Faith of our fathers! Holy faith!*
*We will be true to thee till death!*

*"Our fathers, chained in prisons dark,*
*Were still in heart and conscience free.*
*How sweet would be their children's fate,*
*If they, like them, could die for thee.*
*Faith of our fathers! Holy faith!*
*We will be true to thee till death!*

JW Fairchild

## Trail Notes 11: For the Love of Creation

What rewards did we get for our long trip? During our stop in an oasis just outside of Salt Lake City, we spent an hour feeding and caring for ducks. One duck captured our hearts, and Kaitlyn painted it, out of the love of creation.

*Duck, by Kaitlyn Fado*

# The Christian Warfare

Original Text

### The Battlefield

The Christian life is a warfare. When the children of Israel entered the Promised Land, they entered not a land of ease, but of conflict; not of peace, but of war. They had to fight for every foot of ground which they took for possession. The Canaanites dwelt there when they crossed Jordan, and were never able to drive them out of the land. When strong, they put them to tribute, but the Canaanites continued to dwell among them, and were "thorns in their sides."

Israel's warfare was not just one battle against the inhabitants of the land, but it was a life-long warfare until they had subdued them and were forever free from those adversaries. Defeated and put down in one section, the enemy would rise up in another and cause trouble. But not always were the Israelites victorious. It was a conflict of uncertain vicissitude.

And just as ancient Israel had to fight in the land of Canaan, so the child of God who enters the kingdom today has a battle on his hands. It is a battle between right and wrong, between truth and error; when we conclude our enemy is dead, or has been converted to our cause, we are badly deceived, and are heading for a heavy defeat.

The enemy is strong, and we meet him, not in our strength, but in the strength of the Lord, if we would be victorious. We are soldiers of Jesus Christ, and as such we must endure the hardness of the soldier's life, and fight the good fight of faith.

In any warfare it is absolutely essential that we know exactly who the enemy is. If we know not our foe, our fight cannot be properly directed. The earthly soldier can recognize his opponent by his uniform, but this is not always true of the Christian soldier, for Satan can be transformed into an angel of light, and his ministers come clad in the uniforms of the righteous. So it is highly essential that we be able to recognize our enemy no matter what garb he may wear and know against whom or what we are fighting.

In **Ephesians 6:12**, we have a fair description of the enemy against whom we fight. **"For we wrestle not against flesh and blood, but against principalities, against powers, against the rulers of the darkness of this world, against spiritual wickedness in high places."** We are not fighting against men. In wars of earth, men line up in battle against men, the flesh is mangled and the blood flows. Men who have never met before, men who have never done each other a wrong, men who have no quarrel with each other, meet in deadly combat, wound, mutilate and slaughter each other. It is a warfare against flesh and blood.

But not so with the Christian warfare. We are fighting against the principle, against the power that produces fights between men, and wars between nations. We oppose not our fellow beings, even though they be bitter enemies to us, but we are fighting against the principle in all of us that makes us hate each other. We are fighting against "Spiritual wickedness in high places, and the high places where that wickedness operates is the human heart. Satan's strongest fortifications, the place where he is most firmly entrenched, and from which it is hardest to dislodge him, is my own heart, and there my Armageddon must be fought.

The foes that the child of God must combat are legion. The world with its wealth, its vanity, its pomp and show, seeks to draw us into its carnal clutches. The devil sets snares, digs pits, uses all his cunning devices to take us unawares. The voice of pleasure and folly lures the heart away.

> *"But of all the foes we meet,*
> *None so oft mislead our feet;*
> *None betray us into sin,*
> *Like the foes that dwell within."*

## Flowers for the Living

Self is man's worst enemy, and he is harder to conquer than all the other foes we have to meet. Some years ago a brother in Arkansas said to me, "Brother Fairchild, there is one person I just will not fellowship." I asked him who that person was. He answered, "an Absoluter." (An absoluter is one who believes in absolute predestination). I did not discuss the question with him as to whether an "Absoluter" should be fellowshipped or not, but I replied:

"There is a person in our church I do not like to fellowship. I want to tell you about that man. He has deceived me more frequently, led me into more mischief, gotten me into more trouble, and caused me more heartaches than all other men on earth, and still I would not want him excluded from the church."

The brother replied, "If he is that kind of man, I do not see why you would not want him excluded from the church."

I said, "Because I am that man and I do not want to be put out of the church."

Yes, life is a warfare, the heart is the battlefield, but what of the armies?

## The Two Armies

No war has ever been waged with only one army. You cannot have a family quarrel with only one party engaging in it. You must have at least two parties to a successful quarrel, and therefore, you must have two armies in a warfare. It is needless to say that these must be antagonistic armies, for only antagonists fight each other.

In the **Songs of Solomon 6:13**, we have this question and answer, **"What will you see in the Shulmite? As it were the company of two armies."** One person, yet in this one person we find two armies. And so it is in every individual who has been born again. In the new birth we come into contact with a new life, nature, or spirit, that did not operate in us before, and this new nature is antagonistic to our carnal, fleshly nature, so that as soon as the work of regeneration takes place in the soul, the warfare begins.

It is a mistaken idea that our carnal nature is changed in the new birth. A birth never changes the nature of the thing born, but only develops the nature it already has. The flesh is not born of the Spirit and changed into spirit. Nothing but flesh can be born of the flesh, and nothing but spirit can be born of the Spirit. Jesus said, **"That which is born of the flesh is flesh." John 3:6**. It was flesh before the birth and flesh afterward. For flesh to be born of spirit would contradict the law that every seed must bring forth after its own kind.

The word "flesh" as used here refers to man's natural spirit and carnal nature, rather than to his material body. Paul calls it the "natural man." In the natural birth the natural man is developed and manifested; in the spiritual birth the inward man or divine nature is projected into activity. So in regeneration the old man is not changed into the new, but the new man comes into the old, and now we have an inner and an outer man in the same person. This does not mean that the child of God is two beings, but that he has two natures; these two natures are contrary to each other, and carry on the warfare which rages within us.

The Apostle Paul calls one of these natures the flesh, and the other the spirit. He says, **"Walk in the Spirit and ye shall not fulfil the lusts of the flesh. For the flesh lusteth against the Spirit, and the Spirit against the flesh; and these are contrary the one to the others; so that ye cannot do the things that ye would." Galatians 5:16-17.** Here we have the two armies in the Shulamite, the natures in the child of God. Who does not feel the passion of the flesh, the lure of sensual, carnal things, the desire to satisfy the lustful nature, and also the pull of the Spirit, the yearning for higher and noble things, the thirst for God? It is the battle between the carnal and the spiritual, between the evil and the good, and these two desires are at issue with each other, each demanding our complete devotion, and each so strong in its persistence, that we cannot live the lives we would. These two conflicting natures so dominate our being that, as Paul says, **"For that which I do I allow not: for what I would, that do I not; but what I hate, that do I." Romans 7:15.**

Who has not vowed that he would not do a thing and then gone and done that very thing? And who has not hated himself afterwards for doing the things which his heart condemns? And who does not at times fail to do the things which he wants to do and knows he should do? And who does not blame himself for his failure to live as he should, and therefore, **"consent unto the law that it is good?" Romans 7:16**

The Apostle Paul makes an explanation of this contradiction in our lives, this doing the thing we should not and failing to do the things we should: **"it is no more I that do it, but sin that dwelleth in me." Romans 7:17.** He does not mean that sin in him does it without his volition, but that his sinful nature which he still possesses pulls him into it against his better judgment and nobler desires. He is speaking of the source of the desires which cause him to do these things. **"For I know that in me (that is, in my flesh) dwelleth no good thing." Romans 7:18.** Nothing good springs from our fleshly, carnal nature. **"Now the works of the flesh are manifest, which are these: Adultery, fornication, uncleanness, lasciviousness, idolatry, witchcraft, hatred, variance, emulations, wrath, strife, seditions, heresies, envyings, murders, drunkenness, revellings, …" Galatians 5:19-21.** Carnality produces these acts, and such acts must spring form a corrupt source. Can you think of anything mean, vile, and sinful which is not included in this list? If there is anything else that springs from our selfish, carnal nature, it is of the same kind as the things listed above.

It is a dark picture; and were this the only picture, it would be a hopeless one. That these things do exist in our lives is certain, but they are not the only forces struggling in our hearts. In opposition to them is the Spirit, with its "love, joy, peace, longsuffering, gentleness, goodness, faith, meekness and temperance." So the battle is between the spirit and the flesh, between love and hate, righteousness and unrighteousness, holiness and sin. Both principles are striving to hold the citadel of the soul, and we are pulled one way by the flesh and the other by the spirit, so that we "cannot do the things that we would." In this conflict we discover the law that **"when I would do good, evil is present with me." Romans 7:21.**

In **Romans 8:22-23**, the Apostle Paul throws much light on this experience. He says, **"For I delight in the law of the Lord after the inward man; but I see another law in my members, warring against the law of my mind, and bringing me into captivity to the law of sin which is in my members."**

**"I delight in the law of God."** That is my experience. I take great pleasure in spiritual service. It is not just something in me that delights in the law of God, but I myself, delight in his law. It is the spiritual nature, the inward man, the Christ in me, that causes me to delight in God's law. And is it not glorious that we have this divine nature that lifts us above the carnal and sensual things of earth into the light and liberty of the kingdom of God? What drawing power has the spirit of love to lift us up into the pure and holy! We sit together in heavenly places in Christ Jesus, we feast on the divine manna, we drink from the fountain of eternal joy, our souls overflow with love, and we are lost in communion with God.

While in this state of mind we are free from strife. There is no enemy in sight, no struggle, no conflict, and we may even conclude that our warfare is at an end. But alas! How that "other law in our members" wars against our spiritual nature, and sometimes overcomes us and brings us into captivity to the law of sin which is in our members. It catches us off guard, it sets its traps for us, and often we fail to see the snare before we feel the smart. We cry out with the apostle, **"O wretched man that I am! Who shall deliver me from the body of this death?" Romans 7:24.**

Do you know what it is to be overcome by the flesh, to be taken captive by your carnal desires, to realize that you have sinned, and to

*Flowers for the Living*

stand guilty before God? Did you ever cry out in the depths of despair and ask whence deliverance can come? Torn by conflicting emotions, driven hither and thither by the cross currents of life, wretched because the good you would you do not, but the evil which you would not that you do? What is the meaning of it all?

The Apostle Paul solves this riddle in one sentence: **"So then with the mind I myself serve the law of God, but with the flesh the law of sin." Romans 7:25.** With our spiritual mind we serve God, do that which is right, but with our fleshly carnal mind we follow the law of sin. This simply means that we are complex beings, composed of two opposite natures, each seeking to dominate our lives, and in the struggle for the mastery they pull us first one way and then the other, which makes it impossible for us to live as we would live. It is the struggle between the two armies of the Shulamite, the flesh and the spirit, and neither has completely subdued the other. The battlefield is the heart, and there these two armies keep up their warfare.

## A Lop-Sided Theory

Any theory that does not take into considerations the dual nature of the child of God, and the consequent conflict between the flesh and the spirit is lop-sided, out of balance, and cannot be true, and here is where the doctrine of sinless perfection is found wanting. This doctrine ignores the fact that there are two antagonistic natures in the child of God; that both these natures must continue in us as long as we dwell in the flesh, and that there is no discharge in this inward warfare. In order to live without sin, as some claim they do, one would have to get entirely rid of one's carnal nature, or be able at all times to keep it in perfect subjection, and never have a foolish thought, (for **"the thought of foolishness is sin!" Proverbs 24:29**), and this no one is able to do.

**"There is not a just man upon the earth that doeth good and sinneth not." Ecclesiastes 7:20.** The writer of this statement did not mean that no man doeth good, rather that all his deeds are not good. In a complex being, composed of two conflicting natures, as is the child of God, both natures are sure to manifest themselves at times. And thus, we have the same person doing both good and evil.

This is in harmony with the statement of Solomon in his prayer at the dedication of the temple: **"if they sin against thee, (for there is no man that sinneth not)." 1 Kings 8:46.** Do those who claim sinless perfection agree with this statement of Solomon? In **Proverbs 20:9**, this same thought is put into a question: **"Who can say, I have made my heart clean, I am pure from my sin?"** This is but a forcible way of affirming that no person can claim he has made his heart clean and become pure from sin.

To those who experience the inward conflict between the flesh and the spirit, it seems impossible to make the claim of sinless perfection, but John gives the reason for this claim when he says, **"If we say we have no sin, we deceive ourselves and the truth is not in us." 1 John 1:8.** Those who affirm that they have no sin, or do not sin, are simply deceiving themselves, and others. But John continues, **"If we confess our sins, he is faithful and just to forgive us our sins."** Why confess our sins if we have none to confess? And how can we have sins to confess if we commit no sin?

These statements by the writers of sacred truth correspond with the experience of those who have lived closest to God in all the ages of the past. All had the inward warfare, and all at times were taken captive by their baser selves. Noah, "a preacher of righteousness," got drunk; Abraham, who received the promises, represented his wife as his sister; Moses, who talked with God, sinned at Kadesh and could not enter the Promised Land; David, whose heart was said to be perfect with the Lord his God, was overcome with lust, and resorted to murder to cover up his crime; Elijah was "a man of like passions as we are"; Peter denied his Lord; Paul testified that **"the good I would I do not, but the evil that I would not that I do;"** and even Jesus when addressed as "Good Master," replied, **"Why callest thou me good? There is none good but one, that is God." Matthew 19:17.** Where we become acquainted with those who claim to be sinless, we

*Flowers for the Living*

discover them to be fallible beings like the rest of us. They are as peevish, and as ready to resent opposition as others. We would not know they are sinless if they did not tell us so.

That the children of God are sanctified, no well informed person will deny; but by no means does this imply that they do not sin. The Apostle Paul in writing to the Corinthians address his letter, **"Unto the church of God which is at Corinth, to them that are sanctified in Christ Jesus, called to be saints." 1 Corinthians 1:2.** And still the apostle tells these *sanctified folk* that he could not **"speak unto them as unto spiritual, but as unto carnal."**

Listen to his description of these sanctified saints: **"For ye are yet carnal: for whereas there is among you envying and strife, and division, are ye not carnal and walk as men?" 1 Corinthians 3:3.** Were these sanctified Corinthians sinless? In them the two natures were in conflict, and the flesh was in the ascendancy.

The word sanctify, as used in the Scriptures, usually means to set apart to a particular purpose, generally to a good use, such as the services of God, but sometimes it means to a bad use. Isaiah tells us that, **"They that sanctify themselves, and purify themselves, in the gardens behind one tree in the midst, eating swine's flesh, and the abomination, and the mouse, shall be consumed together." Isaiah 66:17.**

The advocates of sinless perfection put the cart before the horse. They have us cleansed first and sanctified afterward. But the apostle put it the other way. **"Husbands, love your wives, even as Christ also loved the church, and gave himself for it; that he might sanctify and cleanse it." Ephesians 5:25.** Note he puts sanctification before cleansing. God first sanctifies his people, sets them apart for his service, and then cleanses them as a preparation for service. So, while sanctification means that we are set apart for a holy work, it does not mean that the sanctified ones have lost their carnal nature, that the warfare between the flesh and the spirit is at an end, and that they live without sin.

Certainly we believe in holiness. In **Hebrews 12:14**, we are told that without holiness we cannot see God. The same truth is set forth in **John 3:3** where Jesus said, **"Except a man be born again he cannot see the kingdom of God."** Holiness belongs, not to the natural man, but to the spiritual; not to the carnal nature, but to the divine. Until a man is born of the spirit he cannot see God, nor enter into the spiritual realm. **"The natural man receiveth not the things of the Spirit of God, for they are foolishness unto him; neither can he know them, because they are spiritual discerned." 1 Corinthians 2:14.** So to have contact with God, to see him, to know him, to delight in his law and hold communion with him, we must possess the divine nature, for those things are outside the realm of the carnal. And as only our divine nature is holy, and God is divine, it is only in holiness that we see God. We cannot see him in carnality.

While it is a fact that we are imperfect, that our baser self wars against our better self, and prevents us from living the perfect life, we should still strive to reach perfection as our goal. Perfection is the standard which God sets for his people. **"Be ye therefore perfect, even as your Father which is in heaven is perfect." Matthew 5:48.** We should always be striving to reach higher ground than that on which we stand. Our goal must be beyond us, or there would be nothing for us to strive to reach. When we achieve our ideal we cease to grow, for then there would be nothing desirable for us beyond that which we have. God gives us a perfect standard and we should strive to attain it, but it is as impossible for imperfect man to live up to a perfect standard as it is for the finite to comprehend the Infinite.

In **Hebrews 6:1**, we are told to **"go on unto perfection."** How could we go on unto perfection if we have already reached it? When we reach perfection our going on stops, for there is no further to go. The Apostle Paul said he had not reached it, that he was not yet perfect, (**Philippians 3:12**), but he **"followed after, if that he might**

## Flowers for the Living

**apprehend that for which also was apprehended of Christ Jesus."** Apprehend here means to lay hold on with the understanding, to interpret the meaning of. Christ Jesus had laid hold on Paul for a special work, and Paul was seeking to understand just what that work was, to interpret its meaning, and to perform it to the best of his ability. And while he never reached perfection here in the service of his Master, he kept "going on," "pressing toward" the goal he was striving to reach. Who can do more?

But if it were a fact that some people do get all the Canaanites out of their possession, that they completely subdue the flesh and live a sinless life, would it not show more grace on their part to let others do the praising instead of proclaiming it to the world themselves? A wise man said, **"Let another man praise thee, and not thine own mouth; a stranger, and not thine own lips." Proverbs 27:2.** When a man testifies in his own behalf, his testimony is always at a discount. Jesus said, **"If I bear witness of myself, my testimony is not true." John 5:31.** What then must we think of those who boast as to how good they are?

True religion speaks for itself: **"by their fruits (not just words) ye shall know them." Matthew 7:20.** If a man is good, if he lives the Christ life, people will find it out without his shouting it from the housetops, or whispering it in people's ears.

Permit me to use a homely illustration. Back in the mountains of Kentucky when I was a boy, we used a great many gourds. There was the water gourd that we used as a dipper; the salt gourd that hung against the wall and contained salt for immediate use; the powder gourd in which the hunter carried the power for his muzzle loading rifle; and the grease gourd in which lard was kept. Tin cans were almost unknown in those parts in those days, wooden tubs and stone jars were hard to get, and when people rendered their lard at hog-killing time, they put much of it in larger, well-cleaned gourds. No need to be told what was in the lard gourd. It showed for itself. The grease always soaked through and showed on the outside of the gourd. Preachers in those days used to say, **"It is as impossible for love of God in the heart to fail to show in the life of the individual as it is for the grease to fail to show on the outside of the gourd."**

How true! Just as the grease on the inside of the gourd always manifests itself on the outside, so the spirit within manifests its fruit in the outward conduct of the child of God. If you have religion, you do not need to advertise it on your hatband. It will show in your life, and those who associate with you will soon observe that you have been with Jesus.

## Interlude: Kentucky Gourds

For those of you, like me, who had never seen a gourd from Kentucky, the heritage is preserved by the Kentucky Gourd Society (http://www.kygourdsociety.org).

The gourd community embraces a wide variety of treatments that bring out the personality of each gourd. The gourd is a vessel that will manifest what is put inside of it.

## Original Text

An admonition which is seldom used, and which many would do well to heed, is, **"be not righteous overmuch; neither make thyself overwise; why shouldest thou destroy thyself?" Ecclesiastes 7:16.**

*Flowers for the Living*

## Our Weapons of Warfare

An army, not well equipped with the necessary weapons of warfare, cannot hope for victory. The kind of weapons we use must be determined by nature of the conflict in which we are engaged. Men who meet in earthly conflict use material weapons; but when we wrestle not against flesh and blood, but against spiritual wickedness in high places, **"the weapons of our warfare are not carnal, but mighty through God to the pulling down of strongholds." 2 Corinthians 10:4**

In war, we have both defensive and offensive weapons. In the Apostle Paul's description of the Christian's armor, practically all of the equipment that he names is defensive. In fact, he calls the entire outfit "armor," and armor is defensive. Let us have his description. **"Wherefore take unto you the whole armor of God, that ye may be able to withstand in the evil day, and having done all to stand. Stand, therefore, having your loins girt about with truth, and having on the breastplate of righteousness, and your feet shod with the preparation of the gospel of peace; above all, taking the shield of faith, wherewith ye shall be able to quench all the fiery darts of the wicked. And take the helmet of salvation, and the sword of the Spirit, which is the word of God." Ephesians 6:13-17.**

The girdle, breastplate, shoes, shield, and helmet, are all defensive. Only the sword is offensive, and it is also defensive. But when protected by truth, righteousness, peace, faith and salvation, we have nothing to fear from the weapons of the enemy. The sword of the Spirit is sufficient to vanquish every foe.

No doubt you are asking yourself why all the weapons of the Christian are defensive. Why are so few offensive weapons to be used? What does it signify in our lives? What is the meaning to us? It simply means that we are not to fight back, that we are not to return the blow. Jesus fully explained it when he said, **"Ye have heard that it hath been said, An eye for an eye and a tooth for a tooth. But I say unto you, that ye resist not evil; but whosoever shall smite you** on the right cheek, turn to him the other also." Matthew 5:38-39. The Apostle Paul throws further light on it when he says, **"See that none render evil for evil to any man."** If a man does you an injury, you always lose by doing him an injury in return. The only way to destroy an enemy is to make a friend of him, and you can never make a friend of an enemy by opposing him. You can never destroy an enemy by hating him. Hatred has never yet been conquered by hate. It can be conquered only by love. To render good for evil is not only scriptural; it is practical. It works in the everyday affairs of life. It makes you victor over the foes without, and also those which are within.

Let us consider some of the uses to which the weapons of our warfare are to be put, and then we shall better understand the weapons themselves. As before stated, these weapons are **"mighty through God to the pulling down of strongholds,"** and there are many strongholds which we need to pull down. Perhaps the greatest of these is selfishness in our own hearts. And you know it takes powerful weapons to destroy the fortification of selfishness. But armored with truth, faith, and righteousness, and wielding the sword of the Spirit in the strength of the Lord, we can dislodge even this enemy from his entrenchment.

Another work of our spiritual weapons is **"casting down imaginations." 2 Corinthians 10:5.** Imagination is hard to keep in its proper bounds, but truth can do it. Think what mischief imagination often plays. Mrs. Jones did not speak to you Sunday so you imagine that she is hard to get acquainted with. You imagine she considers herself better than you, and does not care to associate with you. But have you stopped to think that *you* did not speak to *her,* Sunday? Was it not as much *your* place to speak to her as it was hers to speak to you? And has not she as much right to believe that she shunned you? It is all imagination, and imagination often needs to be cast down, and truth and soberness set up in its place.

## Flowers for the Living

Then there are those high things **"that exalt themselves against the knowledge of God."** Sometimes the spirit of the Pharisee takes possession of us; we feel ourselves wiser and better than the common herd, and in our hearts thank God we are not like them. We unconsciously assume that "I-am-holier-than-thou" attitude, and thus draw a circle about us that shuts the humble, meek and lowly out. No matter what concern we may manifest in others, what sacrifices we may make for them, as long as there is any feeling of condescension on our part, we will naturally drive others away from us. This feeling of superiority is one of the most blighting, devastating sins that find lodging in the human heart, and it needs heroic resistance.

Again, there are thoughts that need to be "brought into captivity to the obedience of Christ." How prone our thoughts are to go astray; when listening to a sermon, they will sometimes wander off and fasten themselves on some business proposition or worldly enterprise. Even in prayer, they have been known to slip away. They are lured from the service of God by the enticements of the adversary, and have to be arrested, taken captive, before they can be brought back. And we cannot bring them back in our own strength; we cannot take them captive when we are unarmed. It is only through the Spirit that the deeds of the flesh can be mortified, and it is only when clothed in the armor of God, and wielding the sword of the Spirit, that we can bring our thoughts into captivity to the obedience of Christ.

Prayers is another weapon we need to take with us. It is one of the most effective weapons of the Christian warfare. **"Praying always with all prayer and supplication in the Spirit." Ephesians 6:18.** How few people understand the power of prayer! What strength we receive when we commune with God. In prayer we obtain mercy and find grace to help in the time of need.

> *Lord, what a change within us one short hour*
> *Spent in thy presence will prevail to make!*
> *What heavy burdens from our bosom take;*
> *What parched ground refresh, as with a shower.*

*We kneel—and all around us seems to lower;*
*We rise—and all the distant and the near,*
*Stand forth in sunny outline, brave and clear;*
*We kneel: how weak! We rise: how full of power!"*

Power comes to us through the use of our spiritual armor. Weapons are worthless if not used when the enemy attacks. Therefore, let us gird on all our gospel armor, and fight the good fight of faith.

## No Discharge

In wars between nations, and in civil wars between factions of the same nation, it is often possible for the soldier to secure a discharge, which permits him to leave the army before the war is ended. But in the Christian warfare, none is released from the army while the war lasts; the conflict is never ended; and there is **"no discharge in that war." Ecclesiastes 8:8.** Certainly the battle lulls, the soldier is not always on the firing line, but it can never be said that the war has come to an end.

This is not very encouraging to the young convert who is fighting manfully against the powers of evil, hoping soon to drive every lustful desire, every selfish ambition out of his heart, and be free from temptation. Complete and final victory over his foes is his goal, and he feels sure he will soon reach it. But those who have been long in the service know that this is impossible. They have had the victory over their fleshly nature so many times, and felt themselves free from its enticements, only to be deceived and taken captive again, that they have learned the defeat of their inward foes is only the end of the battle, but not of the way. All they can hope for is to bind the enemy and imprison him, rendering him harmless for a while but they know they cannot destroy him.

The mighty soldiers of the cross in the past did not get a discharge from this war. And not only did they fail to get a discharge, but they lost many battles. Noah suffered a defeat after he had come out of the ark; Moses lost a battle on the border of the Promised Land, and was

*Flowers for the Living*

never able to enter it; King Saul lost in his last fight; the sword never departed from David's house; and King Solomon went down in inglorious defeat. The Apostle Paul made three applications for a discharge, but was denied each time. He said he besought the Lord thrice that the messenger of Satan might depart from him **(2 Corinthians 12:8)**, but instead of its removal he was given the assurance that God's grace was sufficient for him. Sufficient for him with all his weakness and infirmities; sufficient in every time of need no matter how strong the enemy, or how fiercely the battle may rage.

If Paul could have gotten a discharge from this conflict, if he could have lived just as he desired to live, if the inward foes had no longer disturbed his peace, do you think he would have felt the need for God's grace any longer? It is when our own strength fails us, when we are losing the fight, that we fully realize our dependence upon God's grace and power. It is in our weakness that "his strength is made perfect;" it is when we realize our own insufficiency that we flee to God for refuge. When we thus see how strength comes to us out of weakness, good out of evil, and victory through defeat, we, too, can glory in our infirmities, that the power of Christ may rest upon us. And we would not ask to be free from a conflict that brings us into closer relationship with our Heavenly Father, and gives us full assurance that his grace is sufficient to save us in every time of need, and his power to keep us to the end of our warfare, when our last enemy shall be destroyed.

No. **"There is no discharge in that war."** We shall have to fight to the last ditch. It is "up hill all the way." But while the conflict goes on we are **"more than conquerors through him that loved us," (Romans 8:37)** and at last when our warfare is ended, and through the gates of death, we leave the field of battle, it will be to rest in peace at home.

> *Brethren, while we sojourn here,*
> *Fight we must, but should not fear;*
> *Foes we have, but we've a friend,*

JW Fairchild

*One that loves us to the end.*
*Forward then, with courage go,*
*Long we shall not dwell below;*
*Soon the joyful news will come,*
*"Child, your Father calls, come home."*

*In the way a thousand snares*
*Lie to take us unawares;*
*Satan, with malicious art,*
*Watches each unguarded part.*
*But from Satan's malice free,*
*Saints shall soon victorious be,*
*Soon the joyful news will come,*
*"Child, your Father calls, come home."*

*But of all the foes we meet,*
*None so oft mislead our feet,*
*None betray us into sin,*
*Like the foes that dwell within.*
*Yet, let nothing spoil your peace,*
*Christ will also conquer these;*
*Then the joyful news will come,*
*"Child, your Father calls, come home."*

*Flowers for the Living*

Trail Notes 12: Achievements

The discussion of Christian warfare puzzled me during the trip across the plains and led me to imagine conversations with JW about how **"there is no discharge in that war."** The picture below, from Kansas, showed the items form a Red Cross package in a POW camp.

Even in this POW package, the needs of community and play reveal themselves, even in the middle of war. So, the conflict continued but the Christian warfare JW discussed focused on the battle for the soul. The passion my great-grandfather brought to the gospel and his themes of following God out of love stayed with me. I considered JW's thought that **"while it pays to serve God, *you cannot serve God for pay.* If the pay is what you are seeking, it is not God, but the pay, that you love."** For the final trail notes I considered the achievements and failures of those generations, remembering that **"the grease on the inside of the gourd always manifests itself on the outside."** JW recognized unanticipated challenges: **"In a complex being, composed of two conflicting natures, as is the child of God, both natures are sure to manifest themselves at**

JW Fairchild

times. And thus, we have the same person doing both good and evil."

**Wall Mural of Achievement**

Trail Trek showed us that the pioneers accomplished much in their struggle between good and evil. At the end of the trail I finally appreciated predestination. I recognize the amount of effort required to make any great event happen. The passion and commitment to God are the weapons we bring to conquer those forces of nature and man that would drive us into decay. Without planning and commitment to the principles of the gospel, or "predestination," there would be no great achievements. The pictures below provide a chart and a map for any achievement. I hear voices ask, "where would your goals and dreams fall on this chart?"

*Flowers for the Living*

**Contributors to Achievement**

On the trail in these conversations with JW Fairchild, I felt the passion in the struggle to achieve things I now take for granted. What an exercise in strength to send mail across the country in just a few days with only a stamp! To make this happen, we needed the Pony Express, a system of national post offices and a culture that could use stamps as a way to trust their fellow citizens and their government. The pioneers embraced the unified America with no tolls to intercept commerce, ponies or the flow of ideas, all because the stamps could cultivate family and further God's work. Those stamps JW sent with his manuscript 60 years ago allowed me to have his manuscript for this trip. JW wanted to communicate across all media his passion for life that he put into his book, and he tried through his manuscript.

Those same community drivers, ideas and passions have driven even more rapid communication where today we are able to talk across a videochat with almost anyone in the world. Those same driving forces lead us to achieve great things for the human community. They can also be used as weapons for evil. As JW makes clear, whatever the ephemeral goals or desires we have, our life on this orb comes down to what we can achieve for our spiritual community. Our job is to shape these ever-changing circumstances to further the changeless laws of the human spirit.

Without such passion and individuals pursuing the love of their God, these achievements we rely on each day would never have happened. My life would be worse.

With the family tour over, we all returned to our life and I gave thanks that JW Fairchild not only left us his thoughts but for his life of passion, struggle and a love of God that has given his descendants many blessings. I had been through half his writings and had loved the companionship. Back in Virginia, I poured a small dose of whiskey and raised a toast to the next time I would engage with JW Fairchild.